# Dinosaur names



Tyrannosaurus Rex
Stegosaurus
Triceratops
Velociraptor
Allosaurus
Spinosaurus
Archaeopteryx
Diplodocus
Megalosaurus
Ankylosaurus
Brachiosaurus
Iguanodon
Parasaurolophus
Hadrosaurus

© 2020

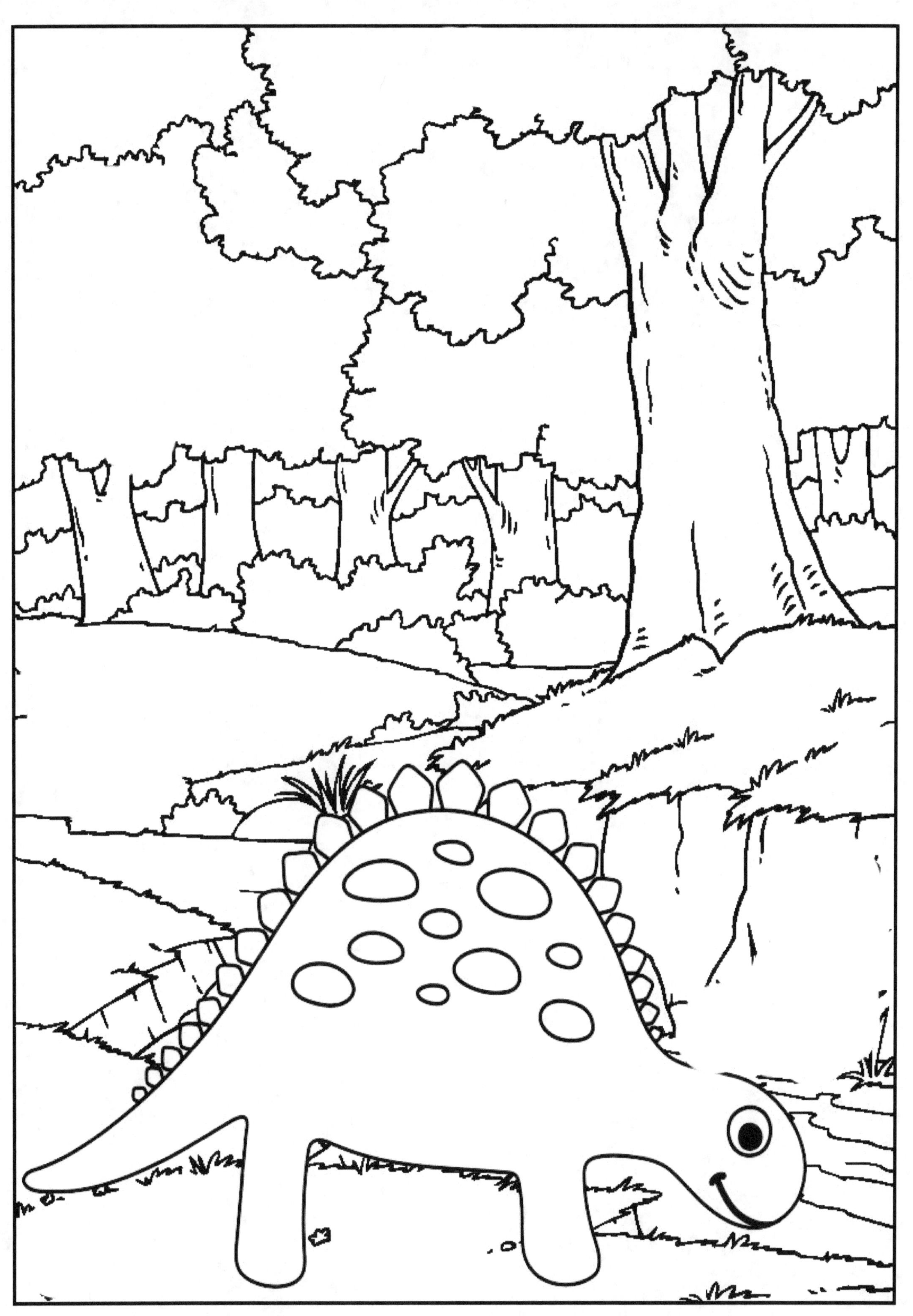

www.ingramcontent.com/pod-product-compliance
Lightning Source LLC
Chambersburg PA
CBHW081322250726
48662CB00008B/2709